THE SUN & MOON SIGNS LIBRARY

AQUARIUS

JANUARY 21 – FEBRUARY 18

JULIA AND DEREK PARKER

Photography by Monique le Luhandre
Illustrations by Danuta Mayer

DK
DORLING KINDERSLEY
London • New York • Stuttgart

Dedicated to Ann Bronkhorst

DK

A DORLING KINDERSLEY BOOK

Editor **Tom Fraser**
Art Editor **Ursula Dawson**
Managing Editor **Krystyna Mayer**
Managing Art Editor **Derek Coombes**
Production **Antony Heller**
U.S. Editor **Laaren Brown**

Computer page make-up Patrizio Semproni.
Photography p 11 British Museum, London/Bridgeman Art Library,
London; p 16 Tim Ridley. Stylist pp 28-29 Lucy Elworthy. Illustration
pp 60-61 Kuo Kang Chen. Jacket illustration Peter Lawman.
With thanks to Carolyn Lancaster and John Filbey.

First American Edition, 1992
10 9 8 7 6 5 4 3 2

Published in the United States by
Dorling Kindersley, Inc., 232 Madison Avenue
New York, N.Y. 10016

Library of Congress Catalog Card Number 92-52794
ISBN 1-56458-094-6

Reproduced by GRB Editrice, Verona, Italy
Printed and bound in Hong Kong by Imago

CONTENTS

INTRODUCING
AQUARIUS

AQUARIUS, THE SIGN OF THE WATER BEARER, IS THE ELEVENTH
SIGN OF THE ZODIAC. AQUARIANS ARE THE MOST
ENIGMATIC OF ALL ZODIAC TYPES, AND ALSO THE MOST
INDIVIDUAL AND INDEPENDENT.

People of this Sun sign have a powerful desire for a lifestyle that is in some way unique. They are often so devoted to it, and so intent on achieving independence, that it is somewhat difficult for them to commit themselves to permanent relationships. At the very least, such a relationship can come rather late in an Aquarian's life.

Traditional groupings
As you read through this book you will come across references to the elements and the qualities, and to positive and negative, or masculine and feminine signs.

The first of these groupings, that of the elements, comprises fire, earth, air, and water signs. The second, that of the qualities, divides the Zodiac into cardinal, fixed, and mutable signs. The final grouping is made up of positive and negative, or masculine and feminine signs. Each Zodiac sign is associated with a combination of components from these groupings, all of which contribute different characteristics to it.

Aquarian characteristics
People of this sign tend to be intellectual and, since the sign is of the fixed quality, you may also be surprisingly stubborn.

Uranus is your ruling planet, and many Aquarians are trendsetters, the leaders of their generation. Perhaps because of the fixed quality of your Sun sign, you can sometimes become a little too set in the opinions that you may have formed when you were young and may consequently lag behind current thought.

Since it is a positive, masculine sign, Aquarius inclines its subjects toward extroversion.

The Aquarian colors are traditionally considered to be electric blue and turquoise.

ARIES · PISCES · AQUARIUS · CAPRICORN · SAGITTARIUS · SCORPIO · LIBRA · VIRGO · LEO · CANCER · GEMINI · TAURUS

FIRE

CARDINAL · EARTH

MASCULINE · MUTABLE · AIR

FEMININE · FIXED · WATER

The Zodiac Wheel

The relationship between each Zodiac sign and the traditional astrological groupings is made clear within the Zodiac wheel. As you read through this book you will also discover references to polar, or opposite signs, and these, too, can be easily worked out by referring to the wheel.

AQUARIUS
MYTHS & LEGENDS

THE ZODIAC, WHICH IS RECOGNIZED TO HAVE ORIGINATED IN
BABYLON POSSIBLY AS MANY AS 2,500 YEARS AGO, IS
A CIRCLE OF CONSTELLATIONS THROUGH WHICH THE SUN
MOVES DURING THE COURSE OF A YEAR.

Was Aquarius originally male or female? The Babylonian name for Aquarius, gu. la, has been translated as meaning both a goddess of childbirth and healing, and "constellation of the great man." The latter is thought to refer to the giant Enkidu, described in the ancient epic of Gilgamesh as a man who grew up in the desert among the wild beasts, who became his friends. He devoted his time to protecting the animals and is often shown watering an ox.

The god of fresh water

In ancient Babylon there was also a god of fresh water called Ea, known as "the god with streams," or "house of the water," who was said to dwell in the city of Eridu on the Persian Gulf. He was normally depicted with water streaming from his arms and hands, but is sometimes shown holding a pot. This seems to be a more likely Aquarian figure.

Later, the ancient Egyptians pictorially associated the constellation of Aquarius with the god Hapi, who watered the ground from two jars held in his arms and was a symbol of the River Nile.

Zeus and Ganymede

Manilius, the Roman writer who, in the first century B.C. set down several astrological myths, firmly suggests that the original Aquarian was Ganymede, the son of Tros, king of Troy. He refers to the earliest Greek myths, in which Ganymede appears to be recognized as the deity responsible for showering the earth with the heavens' rain.

The popular myth of Ganymede describes him as the most beautiful boy alive and goes on to relate how Zeus, king of the gods, fell in love with him. Turning himself into an eagle, Zeus carried the boy off to be his cup-bearer, who would pour wine,

Worshipping Ea

The Babylonian water god, Ea, whose name means "house of the water," seems a likely candidate for one of the earliest characters to prefigure Aquarius.

not water, for the gods from a golden bowl. When King Tros quite understandably protested, Zeus sent him two fine horses as compensation, and explained that his son would now be an immortal, exempt from the pains of old age.

The symbol of Ganymede

Although in the Middle Ages Ganymede became renowned as the symbol of homosexual love, during the Renaissance his flight to heaven came to symbolize the soul's ascent to the absolute.

The Age of Aquarius

One modern myth might be said to be the Age of Aquarius, which was made notorious through the radical 1960s musical *Hair*.

Every 2,500 years the Earth passes through a sign of the Zodiac, and these periods are known as ages. The Age of Aquarius may have started a century ago, or it may not begin for another century – opinions differ. One thing that can, however, be said with certainty is that few signs so frequently confer such romantic good looks on their subjects.

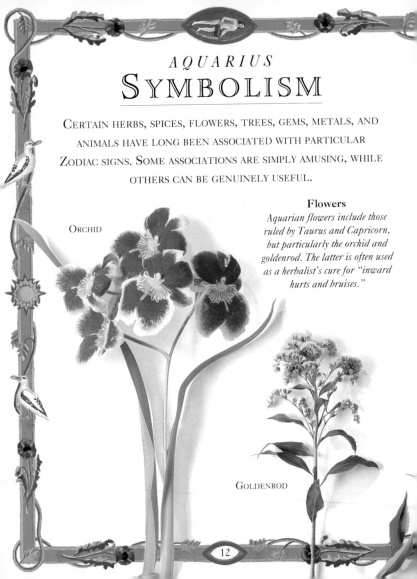

SYMBOLISM

CERTAIN HERBS, SPICES, FLOWERS, TREES, GEMS, METALS, AND
ANIMALS HAVE LONG BEEN ASSOCIATED WITH PARTICULAR
ZODIAC SIGNS. SOME ASSOCIATIONS ARE SIMPLY AMUSING, WHILE
OTHERS CAN BE GENUINELY USEFUL.

Flowers

*Aquarian flowers include those
ruled by Taurus and Capricorn,
but particularly the orchid and
goldenrod. The latter is often used
as a herbalist's cure for "inward
hurts and bruises."*

ORCHID

GOLDENROD

Trees
*Most fruit trees, such as the pear
and the peach, are said to be
ruled by Aquarius.*

ELDER

PEAR TREE

Spices
*No spice is particularly
associated with Aquarius,
but cinnamon, which is
used to flavor apples and
other fruit, and pepper are
sometimes mentioned.*

Herbs
*Taurean herbs are, for the
most part, also ruled
by Aquarius. This is
particularly true of common
sorrel, which helps counter
inflammations, and elder.*

PEPPER

CINNAMON

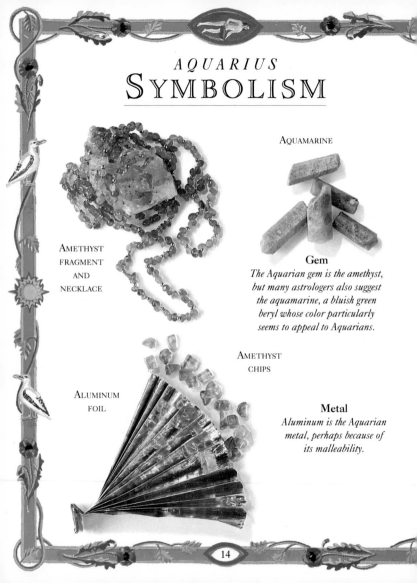

AQUARIUS
SYMBOLISM

AQUAMARINE

AMETHYST
FRAGMENT
AND
NECKLACE

Gem
The Aquarian gem is the amethyst,
but many astrologers also suggest
the aquamarine, a bluish green
beryl whose color particularly
seems to appeal to Aquarians.

AMETHYST
CHIPS

ALUMINUM
FOIL

Metal
Aluminum is the Aquarian
metal, perhaps because of
its malleability.

Animals
*Large, far-flying birds,
especially those that migrate
over great distances, are
ruled by Aquarius.*

EAGLE
FEATHERS

GOOSE
FEATHERS

LEAD
ALBATROSS

AQUARIUS
PROFILE

DUE TO THE FACT THAT AQUARIANS ARE SO INDIVIDUALISTIC, IT IS
VERY DIFFICULT TO GENERALIZE ABOUT THEM. THEY ARE
USUALLY FAIRLY LANKY AND, ON THE WHOLE, TEND TO HOLD
THEMSELVES WELL WHEN STANDING OR WALKING.

The Aquarian stance is usually very correct. You may use your hands to gesture in an elegant, somewhat superior way, and you hold your head high, in order to make the most of your height.

The body

Perhaps because Aquarius is an air sign, the Aquarian body gives an overall impression of lightness, even if you are overweight. Many Aquarians are rather lanky, although their bones are usually fairly well covered by flesh. You no doubt have an upright, erect carriage, with a long back and narrow waist.

Aquarian shoulders tend to be square and broad, and the body joints are prominent. Your ankles will be trim and elegant, with a high calf, and

The Aquarian face
Fine, neatly styled hair and pale eyes characterize the Aquarian face.

your arms and hands are perhaps longer than most people's. There is probably a certain fineness to your bone structure; your features are likely to have a chiseled appearance, as opposed to the more rounded features of, for instance, Librans and Taureans, both of which are ruled by Venus. In fact, curves are very unlikely to play a large part in the make-up of an Aquarian body. It will instead be based upon lines and geometric masses.

The face

Your hair is probably fine, well cared for, and carefully styled, and your forehead is likely to be broad and open. Aquarian eyes are typically pale

The Aquarian stance

A very correct and upright stance is characteristic of many Aquarians. They may appear to possess a certain dignity.

and may have slightly drooping lids. There is a chance that your nose may be a little on the large side, perhaps even a shade imperious; a well-shaped mouth, ready to offer a friendly smile, is also a typical Aquarian characteristic. Your chin may add dignity to your whole face.

Style

Aquarian style is very up to the minute, although some of you may cling to a look that you decided suited you years ago. This is because Aquarians become less adaptable as they age and feel most at home in the initial style that they feel defines them. You may go all out to shock, or use your originality to make a very interesting statement. Pale turquoise or "Aquarian blue" is really your color, and smooth fabrics with satin or silky textures, as opposed to rough ones, will probably suit you best.

In general

Because its subjects are so individualistic, it is very difficult to generalize about this sign. Aquarians

usually carry themselves well, giving the impression that they are somewhat superior or even noble.

There is a certain wildness about some Aquarians. This can manifest itself in the the way they dress – they may, for instance, find some small way in which to bend the rules of a particular dress code. Other Aquarians are, however, impeccably neat and rather conventional.

AQUARIUS
PERSONALITY

AQUARIANS ARE THE INDIVIDUALISTS OF THE ZODIAC. YOU CAN BE
INVENTIVE AND UNIQUE, BUT ALSO STUBBORN AND,
AT TIMES, UNPREDICTABLE; YOU ARE FRIENDLY, KIND, AND
HUMANITARIAN, BUT ALSO VERY PRIVATE.

The only thing two Aquarians will agree upon when reading a list of characteristics of their Sun sign is that they share none of them. This is chiefly because Aquarians are the individualists of the Zodiac and, either consciously or unconsciously, they like to make this known. Because of a perverse streak, they will enjoy being as different from their Sun sign brothers and sisters as they are from other people. Nevertheless, they do share certain characteristics.

At work
Your ideal career will include a good deal of human contact. Because of your happy, kind, and caring attitude, you might make an excellent social worker. Furthermore, you will not find it hard to distance yourself from suffering and will be of real assistance in difficult situations. A large number of Aquarians seem to veer toward careers that are based in the sciences.

You may be involved in the development of communication techniques, or in some other field where a degree of inventiveness and originality is needed.

From time to time, real brilliance can emerge from members of this sign, and anyone close to such individuals should be careful not to write them off as harmless eccentrics.

Your attitudes
It is very difficult to talk of "knowing" an Aquarian; while people of this sign make very good, kind, and helpful friends, it usually becomes clear that because they are so private no one really knows very much about them. If they are questioned (which will seem like prying to many Aquarians) they will very kindly but firmly ease their way out of providing an answer, and put the inquisitors firmly in their place without them even noticing it.

Uranus rules Aquarius

Uranus, a rather unattractive mythical figure, represents the Aquarian ruling planet. It can make its subjects original, versatile, and independent, but also perverse and rebellious.

You will occupy your spare time in a variety of ways, perhaps by going to lectures, rehearsing with a local drama group, or even working on a local charity committee.

The overall picture

There is a tendency among Sun sign Aquarians to be forward-looking when they are young, but to become rather set in their opinions as they get older. It can be very difficult to encourage them to reassess their outlook.

Aquarians are inventive and should develop their potential originality, since they can be very creative. The need to have a distinctly individual lifestyle, as well as overall independence, is likely to provide a great motivation in your life.

AQUARIUS
ASPIRATIONS

YOU LOVE WORKING WITH OTHER PEOPLE, SO THE SOCIAL SERVICES
MAY APPEAL TO YOU. HOWEVER, YOU ALSO NEED SPACE TO
DO THINGS YOUR WAY. AS LONG AS YOUR COLLEAGUES DO NOT
CROWD YOU, YOU WORK WELL WITH THEM.

Science
*The branches of science that allow
experimentation, the expression of
originality, and creative flair, are those that
Aquarians find most rewarding.*

ARTIST'S
MATERIALS

SCIENTIFIC IMPLEMENTS

The fine arts
*An Aquarian who is
attracted to the fine arts will
produce original and very
imaginative work. It may be
spiced with eccentricity.*

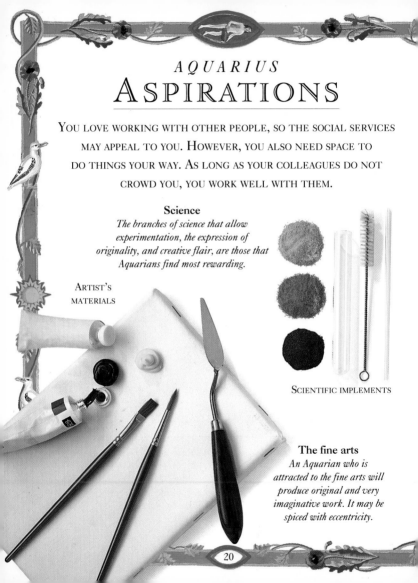

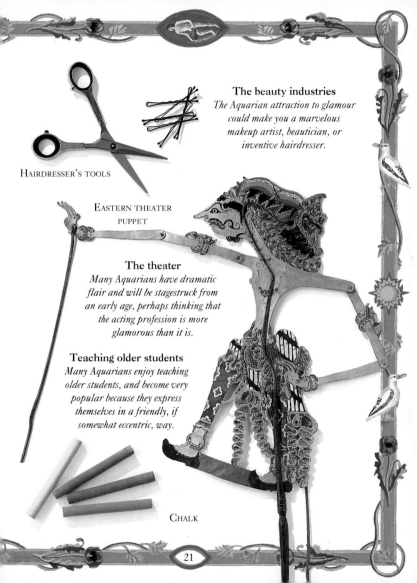

The beauty industries
The Aquarian attraction to glamour could make you a marvelous makeup artist, beautician, or inventive hairdresser.

HAIRDRESSER'S TOOLS

EASTERN THEATER
PUPPET

The theater
Many Aquarians have dramatic flair and will be stagestruck from an early age, perhaps thinking that the acting profession is more glamorous than it is.

Teaching older students
Many Aquarians enjoy teaching older students, and become very popular because they express themselves in a friendly, if somewhat eccentric, way.

CHALK

AQUARIUS
HEALTH

AQUARIANS TEND TO SUFFER FROM STIFFNESS OF THE JOINTS, WHICH CAN LEAD TO ARTHRITIS. IT IS THEREFORE ESSENTIAL THAT YOU SHOULD KEEP MOVING AND GET IMMEDIATE TREATMENT FOR ANY SPORTS INJURIES.

While the ankles are the traditional Aquarian body area, and they are certainly vulnerable, another tradition suggests that joint pains can be a problem. Most Aquarians like keeping active, and it is important that they do so.

Your diet
Natrum muriaticum in its crude form is simple salt, and you may benefit from including it in your diet.

Remember, however, that a balanced diet should give you all the salt you need. Do not oversalt your food.

Taking care
The circulation is Aquarian-ruled, and you may enjoy cold, crisp weather, but make sure that you keep warm.

Because Aquarians need a lifestyle that is unique to their own rather special needs, they tend to become ill if something conflicts with this urge. Should you find yourself falling ill without quite understanding why, or if you seem to be catching every minor infection that is going around, you should take a close look at your lifestyle – unease about this could be lowering your resistance.

Apples
Foods that preserve well, such as apples and citrus fruits, are traditionally ruled by Aquarius.

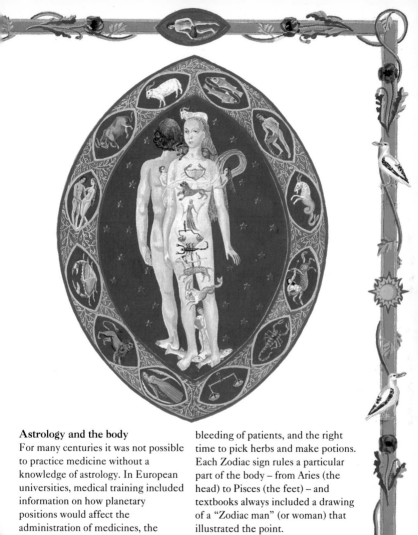

Astrology and the body

For many centuries it was not possible to practice medicine without a knowledge of astrology. In European universities, medical training included information on how planetary positions would affect the administration of medicines, the bleeding of patients, and the right time to pick herbs and make potions. Each Zodiac sign rules a particular part of the body – from Aries (the head) to Pisces (the feet) – and textbooks always included a drawing of a "Zodiac man" (or woman) that illustrated the point.

AQUARIUS AT LEISURE

EACH OF THE SUN SIGNS TRADITIONALLY SUGGESTS SPARE-TIME
ACTIVITIES, HOBBIES, AND VACATION SPOTS.
ALTHOUGH THESE ARE ONLY SUGGESTIONS, THEY OFTEN WORK
OUT WELL FOR AQUARIANS.

Archeology
*An attraction to the deep past often
encourages Aquarians to become
archeologists. This profession enables
them to combine inspiration with
practical research.*

ANCIENT
COLUMBIAN
ARTEFACTS

Ballooning
*Aquarius is an air sign, and its
subjects love unpolluted fresh air.
The idea of taking off in a balloon
or glider could therefore be
extremely attractive to them.*

CIGARETTE CARDS
SHOWING BALLOONING

Collecting old cars
*Many Aquarians are attracted to unusual
hobbies, and some of them enjoy the
challenge of restoring and driving old cars.*

MODEL OF 1930s BENTLEY

FACE MASKS

Drama
*Like those of their polar sign, Leo, most
Aquarians enjoy taking center stage.
Amateur theatricals are therefore
a popular leisure activity.*

Travel
*You will relish the thought of boarding a plane
bound for Iran, Israel, Syria, Russia or Sweden,
and will love flying. You will be eager to savor new
experiences, and may prefer to avoid package tours.*

POSTAGE
STAMPS

Astronomy
*Many Aquarians make excellent
astronomers. The combination of science
and the wonder of the universe is a great
source of inspiration.*

CALCULATING TOOLS

AQUARIUS IN
LOVE

AQUARIANS ARE KNOWN TO BE ROMANTIC BUT CAUTIOUS. THEY
CAN BE COOL, GLAMOROUS, AND ATTRACTIVE, WITH
MAGNETIC PERSONALITIES. THE ACT OF FALLING IN LOVE IS AN
ESPECIALLY MEANINGFUL EXPERIENCE FOR AN AQUARIAN.

When Aquarians fall in love they are, perhaps more than any other Zodiac type, confronted with some very specific problems.

Unless you are very young you will be intent on building a lifestyle that is in some way unique, which you will be reluctant to disturb. This relates to your need for privacy, and to the fiery independent streak that persuades you to live your life in your own particular way.

Partnership clearly signifies that a great deal of change will occur in one's life; in your case, this might mean a measure of sacrifice. This can sometimes be a rather heavy burden for Aquarians, and it is the reason why many of them frequently put off marriage or forming a permanent relationship until quite late in their lives. Very often this is not a bad thing, since it can prevent a series of relationship breakdowns and a lot of unenviable heartache.

As a lover

Enjoyment of love and sex is extremely unlikely to be a problem for you. Even so, you will always be inclined to put a distance between yourself and your partners. You will, of course, want to

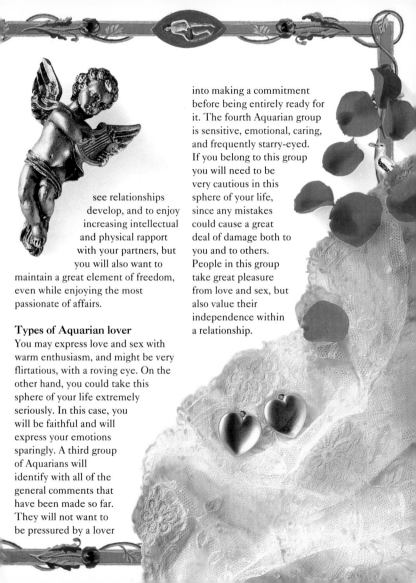

into making a commitment before being entirely ready for it. The fourth Aquarian group is sensitive, emotional, caring, and frequently starry-eyed. If you belong to this group you will need to be very cautious in this sphere of your life, since any mistakes could cause a great deal of damage both to you and to others. People in this group take great pleasure from love and sex, but also value their independence within a relationship.

see relationships develop, and to enjoy increasing intellectual and physical rapport with your partners, but you will also want to maintain a great element of freedom, even while enjoying the most passionate of affairs.

Types of Aquarian lover

You may express love and sex with warm enthusiasm, and might be very flirtatious, with a roving eye. On the other hand, you could take this sphere of your life extremely seriously. In this case, you will be faithful and will express your emotions sparingly. A third group of Aquarians will identify with all of the general comments that have been made so far. They will not want to be pressured by a lover

AQUARIUS AT
HOME

AQUARIAN INDIVIDUALITY WILL PROCLAIM ITSELF IN YOUR HOME.
DO NOT, HOWEVER, FURNISH IT SO TRENDILY THAT IT WILL
LOOK DATED IN A FEW YEARS. YOU MAY POSSESS A TALENT FOR
CREATING ORIGINAL LIGHTING EFFECTS.

Most Aquarians are quite capable of organizing their lives to meet with the requirements of any particular environment. They are therefore equally at home living in either the country or a big city. Even if their dwelling place is quite small, they will make it feel spacious.

Furniture
Aquarians need a feeling of space, so there will probably be as little furniture as possible in your home.

The pieces that you choose are often somewhat clinical in design and usually very modern. If they are not modern items, they will probably have originated in the 1920s or 1930s, when slickness of line and a minimum of decoration were preferred.

Since Aquarius is an air sign, heaviness and too much solidity in furniture is not usually favored. Therefore glass dining tables or

Unique ornaments
Any ornaments in an Aquarian home are likely to be unusual, perhaps because of the owner's interest in the past.

occasional tables are likely to be in evidence. It is, however, surprising how comfortable an insubstantial, angular Aquarian chair can be.

Soft furnishings

While soft furnishings do not usually abound in the Aquarian home, they most certainly add a considerable, possibly Hollywood-style, glamour to it. Aquarians love shiny fabrics, so taffetas and silks are popular among them. Transparent net curtains, or attractive blinds, pulled over only when the sunlight becomes uncomfortable, may also be apparent.

White is a very popular choice for plain walls, and it is sometimes the color used for leather furniture. It is often combined with shiny chrome, which forms the basic structure of tables and chairs. Generally, Aquarians prefer plain or striped fabrics to elaborate patterns.

Decorative objects

All kinds of glass will probably have honored places in your home. You will favor tinted vases, pieces of crystal, and Lalique or other sophisticated glass ornaments. The paintings that you are likely to prefer will be abstract and intellectually demanding, and therefore unlikely to bore you, even after many years.

Since Aquarians are often attracted to the deep past and the distant future, fossils or antiquities may have a place in a well-displayed collection. Nearly all Aquarians love mirrors; they have an unfortunate reputation for being a little vain.

Display of frosted glass fruit
Trendy and glamorous are two words frequently used to describe the Aquarian home. Glass of all kinds is very popular.

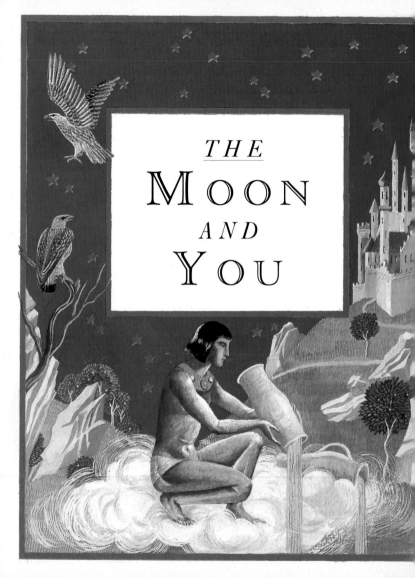

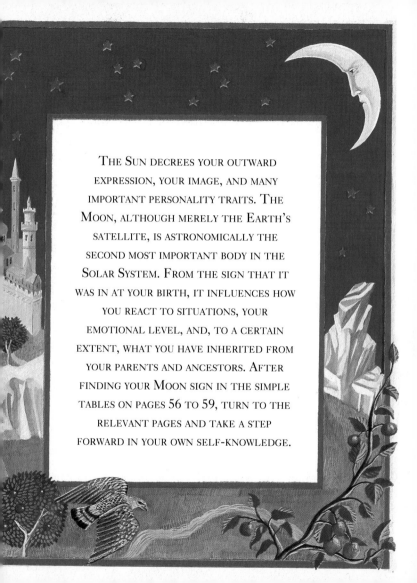

THE SUN DECREES YOUR OUTWARD
EXPRESSION, YOUR IMAGE, AND MANY
IMPORTANT PERSONALITY TRAITS. THE
MOON, ALTHOUGH MERELY THE EARTH'S
SATELLITE, IS ASTRONOMICALLY THE
SECOND MOST IMPORTANT BODY IN THE
SOLAR SYSTEM. FROM THE SIGN THAT IT
WAS IN AT YOUR BIRTH, IT INFLUENCES HOW
YOU REACT TO SITUATIONS, YOUR
EMOTIONAL LEVEL, AND, TO A CERTAIN
EXTENT, WHAT YOU HAVE INHERITED FROM
YOUR PARENTS AND ANCESTORS. AFTER
FINDING YOUR MOON SIGN IN THE SIMPLE
TABLES ON PAGES 56 TO 59, TURN TO THE
RELEVANT PAGES AND TAKE A STEP
FORWARD IN YOUR OWN SELF-KNOWLEDGE.

THE MOON IN
ARIES

YOUR AQUARIAN NEED FOR INDEPENDENCE IS HEIGHTENED BY YOUR ARIEN MOON. YOU ARE ALSO LIKELY TO BE A VERY WARM, PASSIONATE PERSON, WHO WILL EXPRESS EMOTION MORE FREELY THAN MANY OTHER SUN SIGN AQUARIANS.

The elements of Aquarius and Aries, air and fire, blend well and, as a result, you respond to most situations with warm enthusiasm. You thrive on challenge, and always want to be well ahead of your rivals.

Self-expression
Your Aquarian Sun gives you originality, which is complemented by a straightforward, uncomplicated approach to life. You are not inhibited by side issues or petty details.

In spite of your natural Aquarian friendliness, you should be aware that your rapid responses may upset other people. It could be that you organize them too sharply, hinting at incompetence on their part. Try to be considerate as well as competent.

Romance
You are among the warmest, and most passionate and highly sexed, of Sun sign Aquarians. Your Moon sign

contributes a wealth of emotion to your personality and also gives you the ability to express it positively.

Aquarius and Aries are both very high on the list of Zodiac people who need independence and freedom of expression, and your partners must recognize this. When contemplating a permanent relationship, make sure you discuss this part of your character thoroughly with your partner.

Your well-being
The Arien body area is the head, and when you are subjected to tension or stress, you may incur headaches. If there is no apparent reason for these, it could be that they stem from a slight kidney imbalance, so get a medical checkup.

An Arien Moon always tends to make one impulsive and hasty. As a result, you could be slightly accident-prone. Make an effort to develop a more cautious approach.

The Moon in Aries

You enjoy sports and most forms of exercise, and should have a fast metabolism. You will therefore probably burn up calories quickly.

Planning ahead

Your originality and flair may well be expressed through enterprise; you may have two sources of income. You could invest impulsively and be attracted to unsound schemes. Keep your Aquarian cool when investing, and seek professional advice.

Parenthood

You are probably a lively parent and much of your instinctive, warm enthusiasm is likely to surface quite naturally in your children's company.

Because you are rather modern in outlook and enjoy keeping in touch with current trends, it is very unlikely that you will end up falling victim to the generation gap. In fact, the situation could even arise where your children may find it difficult to keep up with you.

THE MOON IN
TAURUS

YOUR TAUREAN MOON MAKES YOU WARM AND AFFECTIONATE IN
YOUR RESPONSES TO OTHERS AND GIVES YOU AN INSTINCTIVE
BUSINESS SENSE. HOWEVER, SINCE BOTH AQUARIUS AND TAURUS
ARE FIXED SIGNS, BEWARE OF BEING TOO STUBBORN.

The characteristics of these two signs are very different, and your immediate responses to situations could consequently be somewhat out of step with your general attitude toward life.

Self-expression

Your Moon gives you considerable stability, and a great need for emotional and financial security. Furthermore, while Aquarius is known for its unconventionality, Taurus has a liking for tradition and a mistrust of change.

Your Moon will encourage and help you to express your originality. It is very likely that you have creative flair of some kind, perhaps for music or singing, and you may want to develop this along traditional, conventional lines. Your Taurean creativity should help you to express your natural Aquarian flair and originality in a very satisfying way.

Romance

The contrast between a need for emotional security and an equal need for freedom of expression will be most marked in the area of your personal relationships. You will place some contrasting demands on your partners. Almost inevitably, you will have to make some sacrifices and compromises, and your lovers must be aware of your different needs.

Your well-being

The Taurean body area is the throat, and it is likely that when you get a cold it will start with a sore throat and end in a cough that is hard to lose.

Most people with a Taurean emphasis enjoy rich, sweet food, and you may therefore be prone to weight gain. Much depends on your metabolism. If it is slow, make sure that you exercise regularly. Also bear in mind that there is a relationship between your Taurean Moon and the

The Moon in Taurus

thyroid gland. If you eat very lightly but still find that you put on weight, get a medical checkup.

Planning ahead

There is a chance that you could be very adept at handling money. You may spend freely on your possessions, and therefore need to earn a good, regular salary.

You have a naturally good business sense and, with Aquarian flair, could do extremely well running a business of your own.

Parenthood

You probably express warm affection toward your children, but may have a tendency to be strict one moment and favor a freer style of parenthood the next. Bear in mind that your children should always know where they stand with you.

Aquarius will help you keep up to date with your children's ideas. However, your Taurean instinct for not breaking the rules may not endear you to them. Make sure that you always aim for compromise.

THE MOON IN
GEMINI

YOUR AQUARIAN ORIGINALITY AND QUICK MIND BLEND VERY WELL
WITH YOUR SPEEDY GEMINIAN RESPONSES AND COMMUNICATIVE
ABILITY. YOU MUST BEWARE OF BEING TOO TRENDY IN YOUR IMAGE
AND OUTLOOK, AND SHOULD NOT SUPPRESS YOUR EMOTIONS.

Both Aquarius and Gemini are air signs, and this element emphasizes an intellectual approach to life. You are therefore more than likely to be in possession of distinctive ideas, logic, and originality.

Self-expression

You should be able to muster your various qualities without much difficulty, although actually realizing your plans may not always be easy; you may enjoy theorizing more than taking practical action.

You probably have a very low boredom threshold, and your inherent versatility will encourage you to learn a little about a great many things. You would do better to study a few well-chosen subjects in depth.

Romance

Neither Aquarius nor Gemini is noted for being able to express their emotions very freely, and this may

inhibit you. You always need a high level of friendship and intellectual rapport with a lover.

Your well-being

The Geminian body area covers the arms and hands, and they are therefore vulnerable. In addition, Aquarians are somewhat prone to arthritis, so it is a good idea for you to have at least one hobby that will keep your hands and fingers very active.

The Geminian organ is the lungs, and bronchitis could trouble you. Seek medical advice if a cough hangs on for more than a few days.

The worst Geminian fault is restlessness, which can impair achievement and sometimes lead to a buildup of tension. A calming discipline such as meditation or yoga will be most helpful.

You probably have a fast metabolism. If you do not, you may need to take regular exercise to fight

The Moon in Gemini

the flab. Fast games such as
basketball, badminton, squash, and
tennis are excellent for you, and you
should also aim to keep your diet as
light and as healthy as possible.

Planning ahead
You probably have the ability to sell
ice in Alaska and will certainly strike a
good deal when, for instance, you
want to sell your car. But be careful:
you may not be as clever as you think
when you have money to invest. Seek
professional financial advice and take

it. If possible, favor a savings scheme
to which contributions are extracted
from your paycheck at the source.

Parenthood
You make a tremendously lively
parent, challenging your children's
opinions and keeping up with them.
The generation gap will therefore
never be a problem for you. You could
sometimes appear a little distant to
your children. Bear in mind that logic
is a good thing, but a warmhearted
hug is also very necessary at times.

THE MOON IN
CANCER

YOUR AQUARIAN ORIGINALITY SHOULD WORK WELL, AND PERHAPS
CREATIVELY, WITH CANCERIAN IMAGINATION AND INTUITION.
IT WOULD BE A GOOD IDEA FOR YOU TO ENDEAVOR TO CURB ANY
UNPREDICTABILITY AND SUDDEN CHANGES OF MOOD.

Your Aquarian Sun and Cancerian Moon bestow some very contrasting characteristics. They can make you a unique, interesting, extremely individualistic, and rather complex character.

Self-expression
You are probably among the most individual of Aquarians. No doubt you respond to most situations in a sensitive and emotional manner, and it is in this respect that Cancer and Aquarius meet most happily.

Aquarians give help generously where it is needed, and do so simply because the need is apparent. They are cool, logical, and rational, rather than emotional. Your Cancerian Moon allows you to be emotionally moved by the plight of others.

At a first meeting, you may give the impression of friendliness tempered by a certain degree of coolness. As acquaintance ripens into friendship,

others will recognize that in some ways you can be quite a softy. But you never lose the ability to snap back when a sharp answer is required.

Romance
In emotional relationships, you may have experienced conflict. On the one hand you have a very deep-rooted longing for a home and family, while on the other there is an Aquarian insistence on retaining your own individual lifestyle.

You respond marvelously to partners and are capable of a really rich and rewarding sex life. Take care, however, that you do not create a claustrophobic atmosphere.

Your well-being
The Cancerian body area covers the chest and breasts. Although there is absolutely no connection between this sign and the disease that bears the same name, it is perhaps

The Moon in Cancer

particularly important for women with the Moon in Cancer to check their breasts regularly just in case there are any problems.

Cancerians are very prone to worry, and Aquarians are detrimentally affected by stress and tension. You may therefore suffer from headaches or even migraines. Learn to relax – yoga and other techniques might well help you to do this.

Planning ahead

You are among those Aquarians who cope very well with money, provided that you allow a naturally shrewd and clever business instinct free expression. Aim to invest in well-established companies and schemes.

Parenthood

As a protective, caring parent, you may sometimes worry unduly about your offspring. At the same time, your modern Aquarian spirit encourages them to be as independent as you are. Be understanding when they decide that it is time to leave home. As long as you curb a tendency to go on about how things were when you were young, the generation gap should not prove to be a problem.

THE MOON IN
LEO

AQUARIUS AND LEO ARE POLAR OR OPPOSITE SIGNS, WHICH MEANS
THAT YOU WERE BORN UNDER A FULL MOON. RESTLESSNESS
MAY BE A PROBLEM, AND YOU MUST AVOID BEING STUBBORN. LET
LEO CREATIVITY BLEND WITH AQUARIAN ORIGINALITY.

We all express some of the characteristics of our polar sign (the sign opposite ours across the Zodiac circle). For Aquarians, this is Leo and, because the Moon was in that sign when you were born, this polarity is strikingly emphasized.

Self-expression
You are a good organizer who is able to take over any situation at a moment's notice. However, you should be careful not to appear bossy. At times, you may seem a little distant and unapproachable.

You may have creative potential, which could be expressed through painting, acting, or maybe fashion designing. Your inventiveness could lean toward a scientific expression.

Romance
You will express your feelings with passion and with all the fire of your Leo Moon. Both in and out of bed,

you will make a rewarding partner. As with all Aquarians, you need a good measure of independence, but you will also want to look up to your partners and be a power behind the throne, as well as sharing it.

Beware of a tendency to dominate your lover; anyone with a Leo emphasis can fall into this trap. Keeping a balance is essential.

Your well-being
The Aquarius and Leo polarity is at its strongest in health matters. Aquarius rules the circulation, which is, of course, driven by the heart – the Leo organ. The two influences combine most potently and call for your special attention. Exercising your heart will assist your circulation, and you must keep moving to avoid any buildup of arthritic conditions in your joints. The spine and back are Leo body areas, and they also need exercise. If you have to spend long

The Moon in Leo

hours sitting at a desk, you may benefit greatly from using an ergonomic chair.

You may like rich food but provided that you keep moving, you will burn up any unwanted calories.

Planning ahead

Aquarians are glamorous, and Leos like the best and the most expensive things. To meet these needs, you will need to earn a relatively high salary. Your Leo Moon may well also give you quite a clever flair for investment, perhaps in well-established companies making quality goods. If you ever need financial advice, you will seek it from the most knowledgeable expert you can find.

Parenthood

Leo is a sign traditionally related to parenthood, and you should get great pleasure from your children, always encouraging them to greater achievements. Always express loving, warm enthusiasm, especially when they show you their efforts. Be rational and forward-looking, and discipline your children positively. You should have no problems with the generation gap.

THE MOON IN
VIRGO

YOUR VIRGOAN MOON GIVES YOU EXCELLENT DOWN-TO-EARTH
QUALITIES. DO NOT LET ANY INHIBITING OR REPRESSIVE
FEELINGS SUPPRESS THE DEVELOPMENT OF ORIGINAL IDEAS
AND UNCONVENTIONAL SELF-EXPRESSION.

Your cool and rational Aquarian Sun combines with the natural common sense and logic of your Virgoan Moon. You are therefore able to look at every aspect of a problem in a critical, analytical way.

Self-expression

You are both original and practical, and should express those qualities fully. They are a source of excellent potential, perhaps for some unique form of craftwork.

You sometimes have a tendency to nitpick, and this can cause you to lose sight of the overall pattern of a situation. Only when your Aquarian Sun takes over are you be able to see the problem in a broader way.

Romance

Your modesty may sometimes cramp your style where love and sex are concerned. However, if you manage to relax into your relationships, you will manage to achieve a really rewarding and ultimately fulfilling love and sex life.

Your well-being

The Virgoan body area is traditionally said to cover the stomach, and you may benefit from a high-fiber diet. Like many people with a Virgoan influence, you could also respond well to vegetarianism. You may sometimes be rather prone to worry, and this could end up affecting your health, via your stomach.

Stress, tension, and a degree of restlessness can lead to migraine if you do not learn to relax. A discipline such as yoga could be of help.

Planning ahead

You will no doubt be as profoundly attracted to glamour as all Aquarians are. However, if you indulge in an excessive amount of glamorous purchases, you could end up feeling

The Moon in Virgo

very guilty. This is far less likely to be the case if the things that you buy actually have a practical purpose of some sort and, even better, if they are made of natural materials.

You may sometimes be inclined to think that you are rather less well-off financially than is in fact the case. While you are generally quite good at managing your financial affairs, you would probably be wise to seek independent professional advice when you want to start saving, or if

you find yourself in possession of a substantial amount of money that you wish to invest.

Parenthood

You could be far more critical of your children than you realize. Be careful, since this could sap their confidence.

Your Aquarian Sun will no doubt enable you to keep abreast of your children's ideas. Make sure that you also provide them with adequate warmth and affection.

THE MOON IN
LIBRA

YOUR LIBRAN MOON HELPS YOU TO EXPRESS YOUR THOUGHTS
FREELY AND WITH ORIGINALITY. YOU ARE SOCIABLE,
BUT YOU MAY NEED TO DEVELOP A MORE SERIOUS, PRACTICAL
APPROACH TO SOME SPHERES OF YOUR LIFE.

Both Aquarius and Libra are air signs, so they blend very well. As a result, you are among the friendliest, most sympathetic, understanding, and diplomatic of all Aquarian Sun and Moon sign combinations.

Self-expression
Your Libran Moon gives you the instinctive ability to see all sides of a problem and to follow another person's argument sympathetically. Understandably, this characteristic can sometimes make you indecisive, and others may occasionally find it annoying because they do not know exactly where they stand with you. It may be worth trying to develop a more down-to-earth attitude.

Romance
Your Libran Moon brings out the real romance that is always lurking somewhere in the Aquarian spirit. You enjoy setting a scene for love. You

will, however, react to your partners in one of two distinct ways. On the one hand, you may feel that you are incomplete as a person when you are not sharing an emotional relationship, and may rush into partnerships. On the other hand, because of your Aquarian independent streak, it is possible that you keep your distance even when a good opportunity arises. You are, of course, capable of building a rewarding and loving relationship with someone who understands you.

Your well-being
The lumbar region of the back is ruled by Libra. If you have a job that involves spending long hours at a desk, you should consider getting a back-support chair.

The Libran organ is the kidneys, and you may suffer from headaches as a result of either a buildup of stress or a slight kidney disorder. If your metabolic rate is unusually slow, you

The Moon in Libra

are quite likely to end up putting on excess weight, so it may prove wise for you to indulge in some regular exercise. You might, for example, consider skiing or working out at a friendly health club.

Planning ahead
You probably love luxury and may well have expensive tastes. Never be tempted to lend money, since you are likely to be a soft touch for unscrupulous people, and take professional advice before buying

stock or starting a savings scheme. Enjoy your money, but keep a firm check on how you spend it.

Parenthood
You may have a tendency to bribe your children for a bit of peace and quiet. This is a bad idea in the long run. Be decisive, and try to be firm, so that your children know exactly where they stand with you. You will be able to keep up with their concerns and should have few problems with the generation gap.

THE MOON IN
SCORPIO

YOU HAVE A POWERFUL EMOTIONAL FORCE WITH WHICH YOU MAY
HAVE FOUND IT HARD TO COME TO TERMS. STUBBORNNESS
COULD SOMETIMES CAUSE PROBLEMS FOR YOU. ALWAYS AIM TO
BE OBJECTIVE AND TO KEEP AN OPEN MIND.

Both Aquarius and Scorpio are fixed signs, which may make you somewhat stubborn and increase your determination in life. This will help you in difficult or stressful times.

Self-expression
You are a typically free, independent Aquarian spirit, but also have all the depth and intensity of a Scorpion Moon and the need to live a really fulfilling life.

You will only be really happy in a career that gives you psychological satisfaction and burns up your great resources of emotional and physical energy. If you do not have such a career, you could stagnate.

Romance
Your powerful source of emotional energy is quite different from your Aquarian qualities. More than any other Aquarian Sun and Moon combination, you need a rich and

rewarding love and sex life. You are passionate and sexually demanding, and therefore require an exuberant and responsive partner. Bearing in mind your Aquarian Sun, you also need to feel free and independent.

The worst Scorpio fault is jealousy – your Aquarian self will hate it if you allow this negative emotion to surface.

Your well-being
The Scorpio body area covers the genitals. Male Scorpios should therefore regularly examine their testicles for irregularities, while women should have cervical smears.

Scorpios enjoy living it up. They are, in many ways, the party people of the Zodiac. Too much rich food and quality wine can therefore result in excessive weight gain among people of this sign. If this is the case with you, make a disciplined and gradual change in your eating habits, however boring you may find this. In theory,

The Moon in Scorpio

you should enjoy sports and exercise. However, unless you are an enthusiast for one particular kind of exercise or team game, you may need variety – water sports, speed skating, and karate should suit you.

Planning ahead

You have a shrewd business sense, and possess what it takes to make a lot of money. This will be useful, since you could well spend money liberally. When investing you may benefit from professional advice, but tell your adviser what your instincts suggest – they could be right.

Parenthood

You could sometimes appear quirky to your children. You may be conventional one moment, and all for a modern outlook the next. Try to let your children know where they stand with you. If you fully express your Aquarian traits, you will have no problems with the generation gap.

THE MOON IN
SAGITTARIUS

AQUARIUS AND SAGITTARIUS ARE BOTH SIGNS THAT NEED SPACE
AND INDEPENDENCE. ALLOW THE WARMTH OF YOUR
MOON SIGN ADEQUATE FREEDOM OF EXPRESSION. THIS WILL
MELT THE COOL DETACHMENT OF AQUARIUS.

The air element of your Aquarian Sun and the fire element of your Sagittarian Moon blend well, making you a very enthusiastic, optimistic person. You no doubt respond with a sense of immediacy and intensity when challenged or faced with a demanding situation.

Self-expression
You are likely to have a positive outlook on life, and will be a free spirit with a wide-ranging mind and breadth of vision. You may, however, cope badly with detail, which might be best left to others.

There is an element of the eternal student about you. You are likely to need an element of intellectual challenge in order to thrive, and should always have some interest that encourages the positive expression of this quality. Although you are a versatile person, you should make sure that you do not spread your

interests too thin, since this could easily encourage you toward inconsistency of effort.

Romance
You have a marvelous source of very positive emotion and probably do not find it difficult to express your feelings. You make a very lively partner, and love and sex are a joy to you. You need a partner who is capable of recognizing your powerful need for freedom and independence, since anything smacking of claustrophobia in a relationship will be fatal to its happiness.

Your well-being
The Sagittarian body area covers the hips and thighs. Sagittarian women in particular often put on weight in this area. To make matters worse, you may have a liking for heavy foods. You should try to lean toward the more typical Aquarian diet of salads,

The Moon in Sagittarius

fish, and poultry. You clearly need a good deal of exercise and will probably enjoy one or more sports.

The Sagittarian organ is the liver, which may well be disturbed by the heavy food mentioned already. You may like taking risks, but should make sure that every one of them is carefully calculated.

Planning ahead

You have something of a gambling spirit and could be excited by moneymaking schemes that sound rewarding but may not be secure. If therefore you cannot resist a gamble,

make quite sure that you do not invest more money than you can afford to lose. Take professional advice before investing; you may make mistakes here from too much optimism.

Parenthood

You are probably progressive and modern in outlook; rational and logical but, at the same time, able to show warmth and tenderness toward your children, especially when they are upset. You will encourage all their efforts and will contribute much to their education. The generation gap will not be a problem for you.

THE MOON IN
CAPRICORN

YOU NO DOUBT HAVE WHAT IT TAKES IN ORDER TO REACH THE TOP,
BUT YOUR AMBITIOUS CAPRICORNIAN MOON MAY TEND TO
MAKE YOU A LONER. YOU COULD EXPERIENCE CONFLICT BETWEEN
CONVENTIONAL AND ECCENTRIC BEHAVIOR.

Before the planet Uranus was discovered in the eighteenth century, Saturn ruled both Aquarius and Capricorn. There are therefore some interesting links between these signs, but also some vivid contrasts.

Self-expression
You will initially respond to situations in a very matter-of-fact, practical way, and will be very cautious. Subsequently, however, your more extrovert Aquarian personality is likely to come into its own. In this way, you will possess a secure basis from which to express yourself.

Capricorn is known for being very conventional, whereas Aquarius is renowned for being unconventional, and likes to surprise and sometimes shock people. You must find a compromise if you are to achieve a balance, and get the best out of both instincts without causing problems to other people. If you are particularly

ambitious, you are likely to lead a very rewarding life and achieve the successful career that you desire.

Romance
Neither Aquarius nor Capricorn is a very emotional sign. You may consciously need to relax into a relationship in order to enjoy a really rich and rewarding love and sex life.

Your Aquarian Sun makes you glamorous and attractive to the opposite sex, but your Capricornian Sun may be an inhibiting factor. Even before a romance begins, you may tell yourself that it is doubtful whether you have found a suitable partner.

Your well-being
The Capricornian body area covers the knees and shins, which are therefore vulnerable. It is important for you to keep moving, and to keep exercising, since anyone with a Capricorn emphasis is particularly

The Moon in Capricorn

susceptible to rheumatic pain and stiffness of the joints. The skin and teeth, as well as the bones, are also Capricorn-ruled.

Perhaps you are fairly lean, with a fast metabolism, and therefore have no weight problem. If this is not the case, you may need to take some regular exercise.

Planning ahead

Your instinctive caution will stand you in good stead, preventing you from frittering money away. You will want the feeling of security that regular savings bring. Although you probably do not need to take financial advice, you should seek it, if only to confirm how good your own ideas are.

Parenthood

You may appear rather cool and distant to your children. While you are kind and friendly, you should make a conscious effort to reassure them in a warm and loving way when they are upset. Be progressive, and you will avoid the generation gap.

THE MOON IN
AQUARIUS

BOTH THE SUN AND THE MOON WERE IN AQUARIUS AT THE TIME
OF YOUR BIRTH, SO YOU WERE BORN UNDER A NEW MOON. BECAUSE
AQUARIUS IS AN AIR SIGN, THIS ELEMENT POWERFULLY INFLUENCES
YOUR PERSONALITY AND REACTIONS.

Should you study a list of your Sun sign characteristics, you will probably recognize that a great many of them apply to you. On average, out of a list of perhaps 20 traits of a Sun sign listed in books or magazines, most people will strongly identify with 11 or 12. In your case, however, the average increases considerably because the Sun and Moon were both in Aquarius when you were born.

Self-expression

You are perhaps among the most independent and self-contained of all Zodiac Sun and Moon sign combinations. Kind and friendly almost to a fault, you have a unique and individual lifestyle that you have developed over the years and may still be refining. You need psychological space but, since you are a very private person, you also need privacy. Even friends who truly love you may not really know you. You are not concerned with other people's private lives, and expect them not to be concerned with yours.

Romance

Your expression of love no doubt fits the general descriptions on pages 26 to 27. You should study the comments on the different ways in which your Sun sign expresses love and affection, since these variations will add a considerable dimension to your attitudes to love and sex. You have an almost magnetic appeal, but your instinctive reaction to lovers is to let them admire you, but to make them keep their distance.

Your well-being

Because the Sun and the Moon were both in Aquarius at the time you were born, your ankles (the Aquarian body area) are particularly vulnerable. There is also a chance that your circulation may not be very good. In

The Moon in Aquarius

cold weather you should keep warm by wearing several layers of light clothing rather than one heavy sweater. In addition, you should take special care of your spine and back. If you stick to a light diet, you should not incur excessive weight gain.

Planning ahead
In coping with finance you will express originality and flair. This may not be such a good thing, because neither of these traits is necessarily effective when it comes to increasing your bank balance. Always seek professional financial advice.

Parenthood
While you should experience few problems with the generation gap, you may not be sufficiently reassuring, warm, and loving toward your children. This can leave them feeling a little insecure. Remember that they may need stricter discipline than you think is necessary.

THE MOON IN
PISCES

IN DIFFERENT WAYS, BOTH AQUARIUS AND PISCES ENCOURAGE
HUMANITARIAN, CHARITABLE WORK. YOUR INSTINCT TO
HELP OTHERS IS VERY POWERFUL, BUT DO NOT LET IT GOVERN
YOUR AQUARIAN DETACHMENT AND OBJECTIVITY.

The qualities attributed to these signs are very different, making you a multifaceted person. Contrary to your Sun sign character, the influence of your Piscean Moon gives you powerful emotion that readily surfaces, and which you can express in a variety of ways.

Self-expression
You are extremely kind, friendly, and helpful – your Aquarian Sun sees to that. However, since Aquarius is humanitarian and Pisces is charitable, you can sometimes be swept up into making considerable sacrifices in order to help others in need.

You have a great deal of creative potential and must express it in a fulfilling manner.

Romance
You are more sensual and expressive in love and sex than many Aquarians. No doubt you fall in and out of love

very easily, since it is not hard for you to identify with that romantic streak that so often lies deeply buried in the Aquarian personality. However, you still need Aquarian space, and an element of independence within your relationships. Equally, you need a strong partner who will encourage you in all your efforts and help to develop your self-confidence.

Deceptiveness is by far the worst Piscean fault. Do not resort to it, especially if you think it will provide an easy way out of a tricky situation. Furthermore, do not be self-deceptive when you fall in love.

Your well-being
The Piscean body area covers the feet, and yours will therefore be vulnerable to all kinds of injury. You will find exercise sandals attractive and comfortable. Pisceans tend to put on weight rather more easily than Aquarians, and you could rely too

The Moon in Pisces

heavily on junk food, or simply may not bother to eat sensibly. This can be disastrous both for your well-being and for your figure.

You will enjoy rather unusual forms of exercise and sport. Modern free-form dance, roller or ice skating, and sequence swimming are all likely to appeal to you.

Planning ahead

Money probably slips through your fingers. You may give away much more than you can afford, which is wonderfully noble, but can cause problems when you are unable to pay

the rent. If you have a regular job, try to find a savings plan to which contributions are paid out of your income. Otherwise, you should always seek sound professional advice.

Parenthood

You will be a rational, sensitive, and caring parent, but must try to curb Aquarian unpredictability, since sudden changes of mind and mood do not go over well with children. You will always be prepared to give your children a hug when things go wrong and should have no problems with the generation gap.

MOON CHARTS

REFER TO THE FOLLOWING TABLES TO DISCOVER YOUR MOON SIGN.
THE PRECEDING PAGES WILL TELL YOU ABOUT ITS QUALITIES.

By referring to the charts on pages 57, 58 and 59 locate the Zodiacal glyph for the month of the year in which you were born. Using the Moon table on this page, find the number opposite the day you were born that month. Then, starting from the glyph you found first, count off that number using the list of Zodiacal glyphs (below, right). You may have to count to Pisces and continue with Aries. For example, if you were born on May 21, 1991, first you need to find the Moon sign on the chart on page 59. Look down the chart to May; the glyph is

Sagittarius (♐). Then consult the Moon table for the 21st. It tells you to add nine glyphs. Starting from Sagittarius, count down nine, and you find your Moon sign is Virgo (♍).

Note that because the Moon moves so quickly, it is beyond the scope of this little book to provide a detailed chart of its positions. For more detailed horoscopes, you will need to consult an astrologer, but if you feel that this chart gives a result that does not seem to apply to you, read the pages for the signs either before or after the one indicated; one of the three will apply.

MOON TABLE

DAYS OF THE MONTH AND NUMBER OF
SIGNS THAT SHOULD BE ADDED

DAY	ADD	DAY	ADD	DAY	ADD	DAY	ADD
1	0	9	4	17	7	25	11
2	1	10	4	18	8	26	11
3	1	11	5	19	8	27	12
4	1	12	5	20	9	28	12
5	2	13	5	21	9	29	1
6	2	14	6	22	10	30	1
7	3	15	6	23	10	31	2
8	3	16	7	24	10		

ZODIACAL GLYPHS

♈	Aries
♉	Taurus
♊	Gemini
♋	Cancer
♌	Leo
♍	Virgo
♎	Libra
♏	Scorpio
♐	Sagittarius
♑	Capricorn
♒	Aquarius
♓	Pisces

	1923	1924	1925	1926	1927	1928	1929	1930	1931	1932	1933	1934	1935
JAN	♊	♏	♈	♌	♐	♈	♍	♑	♉	♎	♓	♋	♏
FEB	♌	♐	♉	♍	♑	♊	♏	♓	♋	♐	♈	♌	♑
MAR	♌	♑	♉	♍	♒	♋	♏	♓	♋	♐	♉	♍	♑
APR	♎	♓	♋	♏	♈	♍	♑	♉	♍	♒	♊	♎	♓
MAY	♏	♈	♌	♐	♉	♎	♒	♊	♎	♓	♋	♐	♈
JUN	♑	♉	♍	♒	♋	♏	♓	♌	♐	♉	♍	♑	♊
JUL	♒	♋	♏	♓	♌	♐	♈	♍	♑	♊	♎	♓	♋
AUG	♈	♌	♐	♉	♍	♒	♊	♏	♓	♋	♐	♈	♌
SEP	♉	♎	♒	♋	♏	♓	♌	♐	♈	♍	♑	♊	♎
OCT	♊	♏	♓	♌	♐	♉	♍	♑	♉	♎	♓	♋	♏
NOV	♌	♑	♉	♍	♑	♊	♏	♓	♋	♐	♈	♌	♑
DEC	♍	♒	♊	♎	♉	♋	♐	♈	♌	♑	♉	♍	♒

	1936	1937	1938	1939	1940	1941	1942	1943	1944	1945	1946	1947	1948
JAN	♈	♌	♑	♉	♍	♒	♊	♎	♓	♌	♐	♈	♍
FEB	♉	♎	♒	♊	♏	♈	♌	♐	♉	♍	♑	♊	♎
MAR	♊	♎	♒	♋	♐	♈	♌	♐	♉	♎	♒	♊	♏
APR	♌	♐	♈	♌	♑	♉	♎	♒	♋	♏	♓	♌	♑
MAY	♍	♑	♉	♎	♒	♊	♏	♓	♌	♐	♉	♍	♒
JUN	♎	♒	♋	♏	♈	♌	♑	♉	♎	♒	♊	♏	♓
JUL	♏	♈	♌	♑	♉	♍	♒	♊	♏	♓	♌	♐	♈
AUG	♑	♉	♎	♒	♋	♏	♈	♌	♐	♉	♍	♑	♊
SEP	♓	♋	♏	♈	♌	♑	♉	♍	♒	♋	♏	♓	♌
OCT	♈	♌	♑	♉	♎	♒	♊	♎	♓	♌	♐	♈	♍
NOV	♊	♎	♒	♊	♏	♉	♌	♐	♉	♍	♑	♊	♏
DEC	♋	♏	♓	♌	♑	♉	♍	♑	♊	♎	♒	♋	♐

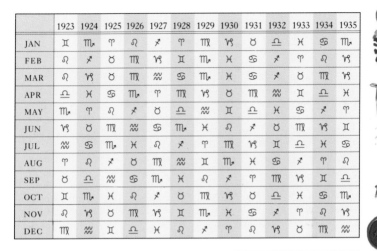

	1949	1950	1951	1952	1953	1954	1955	1956	1957	1958	1959	1960	1961
JAN	♑	♊	♎	♓	♋	♏	♈	♌	♑	♉	♍	♒	♋
FEB	♓	♋	♐	♈	♍	♑	♉	♎	♒	♊	♏	♈	♌
MAR	♓	♋	♐	♉	♍	♑	♊	♏	♓	♋	♏	♈	♌
APR	♉	♍	♒	♊	♎	♓	♋	♐	♈	♌	♑	♊	♎
MAY	♊	♎	♓	♋	♐	♈	♍	♑	♉	♎	♒	♋	♏
JUN	♌	♐	♈	♍	♑	♊	♎	♓	♋	♐	♈	♌	♑
JUL	♍	♑	♊	♎	♓	♋	♏	♈	♌	♑	♉	♍	♒
AUG	♏	♓	♋	♐	♈	♍	♑	♉	♎	♒	♊	♏	♈
SEP	♐	♈	♍	♑	♊	♎	♒	♋	♐	♈	♌	♑	♊
OCT	♑	♊	♎	♓	♋	♏	♓	♌	♑	♉	♍	♒	♋
NOV	♓	♋	♏	♈	♍	♑	♉	♎	♒	♊	♏	♈	♌
DEC	♈	♌	♑	♊	♎	♒	♊	♏	♓	♌	♐	♉	♍

	1962	1963	1964	1965	1966	1967	1968	1969	1970	1971	1972	1973	1974
JAN	♏	♓	♌	♐	♈	♍	♑	♊	♎	♒	♋	♐	♈
FEB	♐	♉	♍	♒	♊	♏	♓	♋	♏	♈	♍	♑	♉
MAR	♐	♉	♎	♒	♊	♏	♈	♌	♐	♉	♍	♑	♊
APR	♒	♋	♏	♈	♌	♑	♉	♍	♒	♊	♏	♓	♋
MAY	♓	♌	♐	♉	♍	♒	♊	♎	♓	♋	♐	♈	♍
JUN	♉	♎	♒	♊	♏	♓	♌	♐	♉	♍	♑	♊	♎
JUL	♊	♏	♓	♌	♐	♈	♍	♑	♊	♎	♓	♋	♐
AUG	♌	♐	♉	♎	♒	♊	♏	♓	♋	♏	♈	♍	♑
SEP	♍	♒	♋	♏	♓	♋	♐	♉	♍	♑	♊	♎	♓
OCT	♏	♓	♌	♐	♈	♍	♒	♊	♎	♒	♋	♐	♈
NOV	♐	♉	♎	♒	♊	♎	♓	♋	♐	♈	♍	♑	♉
DEC	♑	♊	♏	♓	♋	♐	♈	♌	♑	♉	♎	♒	♊

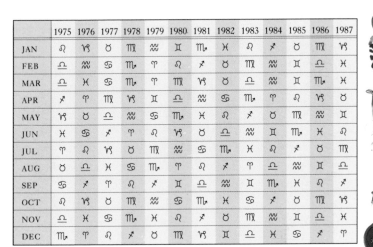

	1975	1976	1977	1978	1979	1980	1981	1982	1983	1984	1985	1986	1987
JAN	♌	♑	♉	♍	♒	♊	♏	♓	♌	♐	♉	♍	♑
FEB	♎	♒	♋	♏	♈	♌	♐	♉	♍	♒	♊	♎	♓
MAR	♎	♓	♋	♏	♈	♍	♑	♉	♎	♒	♊	♏	♓
APR	♐	♈	♍	♑	♊	♎	♒	♋	♏	♈	♌	♑	♉
MAY	♑	♉	♎	♒	♋	♏	♓	♌	♐	♉	♍	♒	♊
JUN	♓	♋	♐	♈	♌	♑	♉	♎	♒	♊	♏	♓	♌
JUL	♈	♌	♑	♉	♍	♒	♋	♏	♓	♌	♐	♉	♍
AUG	♉	♎	♓	♋	♏	♈	♌	♐	♈	♎	♒	♊	♎
SEP	♋	♐	♈	♌	♐	♊	♎	♒	♊	♏	♓	♌	♐
OCT	♌	♑	♉	♍	♒	♋	♏	♓	♋	♐	♉	♍	♑
NOV	♎	♓	♋	♏	♓	♌	♐	♉	♍	♒	♊	♎	♓
DEC	♏	♈	♌	♐	♉	♍	♑	♊	♎	♓	♋	♐	♈

	1988	1989	1990	1991	1992	1993	1994	1995	1996	1997	1998	1999	2000
JAN	♊	♎	♒	♋	♏	♈	♌	♑	♉	♎	♒	♊	♏
FEB	♋	♐	♈	♍	♑	♉	♎	♒	♋	♏	♈	♌	♐
MAR	♌	♐	♉	♍	♒	♊	♎	♓	♋	♏	♈	♌	♑
APR	♍	♒	♊	♏	♓	♋	♐	♈	♍	♑	♊	♎	♓
MAY	♏	♓	♌	♐	♈	♍	♑	♉	♎	♒	♋	♏	♈
JUN	♐	♉	♍	♑	♊	♎	♓	♋	♐	♈	♌	♑	♉
JUL	♑	♊	♎	♒	♋	♐	♈	♌	♑	♉	♎	♒	♋
AUG	♓	♌	♐	♈	♍	♑	♉	♎	♓	♋	♏	♓	♌
SEP	♉	♍	♑	♊	♏	♓	♋	♏	♈	♌	♑	♉	♎
OCT	♊	♎	♒	♋	♐	♈	♌	♑	♉	♎	♒	♊	♏
NOV	♌	♐	♈	♍	♑	♉	♎	♒	♋	♏	♈	♌	♑
DEC	♍	♑	♉	♎	♒	♋	♏	♈	♌	♐	♉	♍	♒

THE SOLAR SYSTEM

THE STARS, OTHER THAN THE SUN, PLAY NO PART IN THE SCIENCE
OF ASTROLOGY. ASTROLOGERS USE ONLY THE BODIES IN THE
SOLAR SYSTEM, EXCLUDING THE EARTH, TO CALCULATE HOW OUR
LIVES AND PERSONALITIES CHANGE.

Pluto
Pluto takes 246 years to travel around
the Sun. It affects our unconscious
instincts and urges, gives us strength
in difficulty, and perhaps emphasizes
any inherent cruel streak.

Neptune
Neptune stays in each sign for 14
years. At best it makes us sensitive
and imaginative; at worst it
encourages deceit and carelessness,
making us worry.

Uranus
The influence of Uranus can make us
friendly, kind, eccentric, inventive,
and unpredictable.

Saturn
In ancient times, Saturn was the most
distant known planet. Its influence
can limit our ambition and make us
either overly cautious (but practical),
or reliable and self-disciplined.

SATURN

PLUTO

NEPTUNE

URANUS

Jupiter

Jupiter encourages expansion, optimism, generosity, and breadth of vision. It can, however, also make us wasteful, extravagant, and conceited.

Mars

Much associated with energy, anger, violence, selfishness, and a strong sex drive, Mars also encourages decisiveness and leadership.

JUPITER

MARS

The Moon

Although it is a satellite of the Earth, the Moon is known in astrology as a planet. It lies about 240,000 miles from the Earth and, astrologically, is second in importance to the Sun.

MERCURY

THE MOON

VENUS

EARTH

The Sun

The Sun, the only star used by astrologers, influences the way we present ourselves to the world – our image or personality; the face we show to other people.

Venus

The planet of love and partnership, Venus can emphasize all our best personal qualities. It may also encourage us to be lazy, impractical, and too dependent on other people.

Earth

Every planet contributes to the environment of the Solar System, and a person born on Venus would no doubt be influenced by our own planet in some way.

Mercury

The planet closest to the Sun affects our intellect. It can make us inquisitive, versatile, argumentative, perceptive, and clever, but maybe also inconsistent, cynical, and sarcastic.